P9-APW-996

Law in the Curriculum

by Murry R. Nelson

Library of Congress Catalog Card Number: 78-50367
ISBN 0-87367-106-6
Copyright© 1978 by The Phi Delta Kappa Educational Foundation
Bloomington, Indiana

TABLE OF CONTENTS

What Is Law-Related Education?

"There should be a law that says 'no fires near anyone's home.'"

"People should be quiet at night. There should be a rule that says, 'no noise at night.'"

"All food should be shared."

"No! Everyone should be able to have what he grows."

Does this sound like the dialogue in a town council meeting? How about in a commune of young people? You might be quite surprised to discover that this dialogue occurred in a classroom of third-graders. They were responding to a very clever film cartoon called "Why We Have Laws—Shiver, Gobble, and Snore," which focuses on three friends who decide to form their own community to escape the tyrannical and capricious rules of their king. They decide to go live in a place where they can be free—where there are no rules. They find, however, that without any rules they are constantly arguing and are unable to live peacefully. They decide that to be truly "free" *and* to live with others they must make rules.

At this point the teacher stopped the film and asked the students to make appropriate rules for the three friends. The students then launched into a sophisticated discussion not only on the needed laws for the community in the film, but on the general need for laws and specificity within those laws.

In a kindergarten classroom the youngsters are hotly debating a question of fairness in a modern version of "The Little Red Hen." Two youngsters wished to bake cookies with a neighbor who said that if they returned the next afternoon they could, indeed, bake cookies. The next day one youngster returned at the appointed time, helped in the baking and cleaning up, then anxiously waited for the cookies to cool. At that point the other child ran up and said that he smelled cookies. The first child, Kim, protested that Kevin should not get any cookies because he failed to help in the baking or cleaning up. Kevin said that he had wanted to help but he had to watch his little sister while his mother took his grandfather to the doctor. It had been a last-minute emergency.

Now the kindergarten students are attempting to determine what is a fair solution for all parties concerned.

In a U.S. history class the teacher is discussing the failure of the Articles of Confederation.

> "America needed a new set of laws because nobody *had* to obey the old laws," offered one student.
>
> "Why were laws needed at all?" queried the teacher.
>
> "Well, without them the states were just like independent countries, taxing each other, coining their own money, and restricting trade."

All three of these cases illustrate a simple beginning to the study of the need for rules and laws. In each instance the teacher used the initial case to develop the rationale for rules and laws—in school, at home, in communities, in the nation. What often follows is an examination by students at various levels of sophistication of rules that are necessary and unnecessary. Students may go on to make their own rules for their classroom or to suggest changes in certain rules affecting all students in the school.

These ideas do not come all at once to all students, but inevitably they do come—even to the youngest of students. A commitment to teach law-related education requires a tacit agreement by teachers to give students an opportunity to live the law, not merely learn about it. Proponents of law-related education see this opportunity (to live the law) as a natural introduction to citizenship education as well as a way of providing experience in a neglected basic skill—the ability to operate within the laws of our society.

Why Study About the Law?

The goals of law-related education can be divided into three categories. Two have been briefly mentioned: citizenship and skills. The third is related to the acquisition of social science knowledge. Each of these goals needs some elaboration.

Many educators now accept law-related education as an important component of training for citizenship. Political accountability has become increasingly important to a populace shocked by scandals like Watergate, the affairs of certain congressmen, and influence peddling in Congress by the South Korean government. The consumer movement has also intensified awareness of the need to understand laws that affect us every time we buy, or contemplate buying, a product or service.

Another argument for law-related education stems from the enactment of the Twenty-Sixth Amendment to the U.S. Constitution, which gave 18-year-olds the franchise. Now students can be prepared to vote intelligently on issues and candidates without a three-year gap between leaving public schooling and the acquisition of majority status. Thus the task of the schools to prepare citizens is more vital today than ever before.

Without an understanding of the legal workings of our society, a sense of helplessness or cynicism may easily set in. Much evidence exists to indicate that such feelings have *already* set in: the increase in the number of serious crimes, the decrease in the number of eligible voters actually voting (in a recent mayoral election in Chicago, less than one-third of those eligible to vote actually cast ballots), the increase in juvenile crime, and the alarming rise in violence and vandalism in schools nationwide. If citizens are better informed, there seems to be a greater likelihood that they will operate within the legal restraints of society.

Another argument for including law in the curriculum is that an understanding of our society's laws is a basic skill every bit as important as reading, writing, and arithmetic. An overly narrow view of "basics" can obscure the fact that all of us must learn at least one other basic—how to get along in society. The importance of the three Rs is not in question, but life in a complex society involves much more. Whether students can balance a checkbook is a direct function of mathematics, and it is important. Equally important, however, is an understanding of what a check represents, what responsibility it involves. Law affects all citizens every day. You cannot get up in the morning, brush your teeth, use the telephone, or eat a meal without being affected by some legal guidelines or constraints. Attaining the skills necessary to recognize and operate effectively within those constraints is a priority of the law-related education movement. Other useful skills are developed through law-related education. These include role playing, decision making, and problem solving. Though not the exclusive province of law-related education, these skills are an integral part of the pedagogy of a curriculum devoted to legal concepts.

Still another rationale for the study of law in the curriculum is that it provides a fitting stage for introducing social science concepts. The concepts of power, justice, scarcity, culture, property, etc., can be viewed against the backdrop of law and made meaningful. Law offers a unique opportunity for students in all grades to study one overriding concept that is universal in all cultures: the promulgation and enforcement of rules and laws.

Law-related education, then, is a movement that has distinct similarities to citizenship education but demands far more involvement of students, teachers, and community than has been the case in earlier citizenship programs. This movement has been quietly growing for over 10 years, but its concerns reflect ideas of earlier educators such as John Dewey, Harold Rugg, and George Counts.

In the early 1960s there were a number of isolated projects predicated upon the idea that students should know more about the law.

These projects were local, mostly urban, and usually small in scale. Their accomplishments and objectives were not widely known or replicated. There was a need for an interested party to act as a clearing-house and disseminator of programs and materials. That need was met when, in 1971, the American Bar Association (ABA) created its Special Committee on Youth Education for Citizenship (YEFC) with a mandate to improve and foster quality law-related programs in grades K-12. The YEFC committee does not produce materials, per se, but instead produces occasional papers and articles informing others of available materials and of nationwide projects in the area of law-related education. These publications are inexpensive and include two annotated bibliographies of law-related education print materials, an annotated media bibliography, an annotated gaming bibliography, a directory of law-related educational projects, a source book for funding, and a volume on inservice teacher training, among other items.

The ABA and many state and local bar associations have been very supportive of efforts in law-related education and should be looked to for continuing assistance by those interested in initiating or furthering such programs. Currently, at least 48 of the 50 states and the District of Columbia have some sort of law-related education. In some cases it may merely be a course in one high school or a statewide legal education observance of Law Day (May 1), but these are the exceptions. Many states have a number of well-developed programs funded by various government and private sources. In California alone, at least 40 district or citywide projects are in operation. In Pennsylvania, for example, the state department of education decided to channel much of the money it received under a Law Enforcement Assistance Administration grant to local areas for developing programs with local organization and input rather than mandate state-imposed and state-developed programs. With that in mind, regional councils were formed to promote various law-related education programs throughout their regions. In addition, the Pennsylvania Department of Education developed and distributes a booklet called *Law-Related Education Competencies,** which has been a valuable resource for schools wishing to introduce law in their curricula.

Addresses for all source materials mentioned are provided in the Appendix.

The inclusion of law in the K-12 curriculum, then, is a relatively recent but rapidly growing movement in education. Developing respect for the law has obviously been a concern undergirding this movement, but just as important is teaching students the rationale for various laws. Direct experience in living the law and consequent social action related to revising or creating laws and regulations are the catalysts contributing to student, teacher, and community excitement over law-related education.

Where Can We Study About the Law?

The first section of this fastback introduced the reader to the rationale for law-related education and has provided some brief examples of how legal concepts can be introduced at various grade levels. In this section I will present in more depth a structure for including the study of law in the K-12 curriculum.

There have been two approaches to the study of law in the schools. One is to offer a separate course or courses in law; the second is to integrate the concepts of law throughout the curriculum. Often this integration is limited to the social studies curriculum, but law concepts can be integrated throughout the curriculum, particularly in the elementary grades. It is my contention that in the elementary school the most meaningful way to present law-related education is through an integrated approach. If one of the main objectives of law-related education is to give students the opportunity to live the law, then it seems absurd to ask them to do this only during a unit of three to six weeks. What seems more sensible is a totally integrated law-related education approach starting in kindergarten. With this approach, the answer to the often-asked question, "If law-related education goes into our curriculum, what comes out?" is, "Nothing." Instead, the law becomes an additional strand to reinforce the concepts and/or content within the present curriculum. An exploration of how this might work follows.

Primary Grades: The primary grades seek to give students basic knowledge in content areas as well as those social and personal "basics" necessary to function comfortably in our society. Students in these early grades must learn whole new sets of rules that govern their conduct in both the classroom and the total school community. Most of the time these rules are imposed upon the students with little or no explanation. In the context of law-related education, this type of imposed rules would be contradictory to learning to live the law. Rather than merely stating rules, the teacher might illustrate the need for rules and laws, as was discussed earlier with the characters Shiver, Gobble, and Snore in the film cartoon. Students can then look at the rules that they follow (and might even help make) in their family. Students might discuss how rules are made and enforced in their family. Can and should the same guidelines govern the creation and enforcement of rules in the school? Rules that are imposed on the family and school should also be noted. Later, students could discover how and why these rules are made. Examples might include why we need licenses to drive, marry, and work, or why we have certificates attesting to one's birth, marriage, or death. Law-related education also provides a natural and logical way to broach a sensitive subject that affects more and more people each day: divorce. Another sensitive topic, adoption, can be discussed and developed in this same manner. Certainly these latter concepts are so common in many children's lives that they can and should be dealt with in a more constructive way. Our laws are certainly a reflection of our societal values. As they mature, students will begin to see the relationships in increasingly complex ways.

Closely related to rule making and enforcement is the concept of leadership. Primary students should be shown this relationship. In a school in Denton, Texas, Patricia Moseley, the principal, has developed with her teachers three concepts in law-related education for K-3 students. These concepts are leadership, fairness, and responsibility, and they are demonstrated through activities in the classroom, the school yard, and in other areas of the school; e.g., a kindergarten class recently invited their school custodian to the classroom to explore the nature of leadership and responsibility in another way. The children discussed with the custodian his work (his leadership in the school). They also learned how they could aid the custodian by such practices as picking up litter, storing equipment in the proper place, and wiping their feet before entering the building.

Middle Grades: In grades 4-8 students usually spend a good deal of time either in specific subject areas or in studying units that cut across disciplines. In the former case, the law is probably most logically studied in the social studies. Almost every state requires or recommends a course in state history and government at some point in the middle grades. In Indiana, Pennsylvania, and Colorado, for example, it is in grade 4. In Texas, Nevada, and Ohio it is in grade 7. Typically such courses deal with the familiar litany of names, dates, and places. The question of rights and responsibilities in state history is frequently overlooked, e.g., in a fourth-grade class in Pennsylvania the students skip lightly over the treaties William Penn and others made with some of the native American Indian tribes. In some classes, however, a teacher uses this topic to delve into the nature of a treaty, its legal status, and its consequences for the future. Students then begin questioning the limitations of those treaties today and investigate other treaties between various countries. The students also ponder the types of enforcement sanctions possible between nations, short of going to war.

Other opportunities for law-related education can be found in the local community. A teacher in a central Pennsylvania community used the arrest of a farmer for shooting deer out of season to initiate law study. The students were assigned to examine the case by reading about it in a series of newspaper articles, then to express their feelings about the laws involved. Two groups were then formed to debate the issues and discuss whether the law involved was equitable and whether some alternatives were possible for the farmer under the existing law. From there the teacher led a discussion of the need for the laws and regulations in question. Other activities followed, since this teacher considered law education a core concept in the study of state and regional history and government.

Other common subjects in the middle grades also lend themselves to law education. United States history, world history, and regional culture studies all have subject matter areas that lend themselves to a law-related approach. The study of the Middle East becomes much clearer when the "laws" of Islam are understood as a matrix of Middle Eastern culture. Indeed, to merely "study" the government composition of a country without attempting to understand the cultural influence on its laws is to neglect the most important and universal factors of national identity.

Social studies are not the only area for law study in the middle grades, however. Scientific issues often have legal aspects. The study of DNA in biology might include investigation of the protests about further research on recombinant DNA molecules. The creation of bigger and better bombs is obviously a result of scientific and technological advancement, but laws and treaties regulate the use and proliferation of such weaponry. Environmental science requires the study of laws regulating practices that have environmental ramifications. There are government regulatory agencies to cover nearly all aspects of scientific inquiry and development. The Food and Drug Administration, the Federal Power Commission, the Atomic Energy Commission, the Consumer Products Safety Commission, to name just a few, are federal agencies with the legal authority to regulate scientific developments.

The study of similar issues could be undertaken at a junior high or senior high level where subjects are departmentalized. The social studies might be better suited to dealing with law-related concerns, but it should not be thought that law-related education is limited to that subject area at the secondary level anymore than it is at the elementary level.

One state, Missouri, has promoted law-related education through a concerted effort in all areas of the curriculum: science, mathematics, language arts, physical education, even art. This statewide thrust has been generously aided by the Missouri Bar Association's work with teachers throughout the state.

Junior-Senior High: Despite the comments made above about integration across disciplinary lines, the bulk of law-related education at the secondary school level remains in separate units or courses. In State College, Pennsylvania, the ninth-grade social studies team at Park Forest Junior High School has developed a seven-week unit called "The Three Rs of Law—Respect, Rights, and Responsibility," which seeks to instill in students the idea that in order to have certain rights, people must exercise responsibility and respect for others' rights. In simple terms, law is a two-way street. The unit examines various aspects of law that affect all citizens, and students in particular. The focus is on basic rights; there is no emphasis on crime, crimi-

15

nal behavior, or the penal system (popular topics in other law curricula) since the school also offers two minicourses in those areas.

Many junior and senior high schools have found law studies courses or units successful in giving students a better understanding of their role as citizens. Students find them challenging and exciting. In a number of secondary schools in Washington, D.C., a course called "Street Law" is taught by law students. The course has spread to many other cities, where local law students come into high schools and junior highs to teach students about criminal law, consumer law, family law, and housing law, among other topics. A similar model is used in the Tucson public schools in their High School Teaching Project. Other models for teaching law units or courses can be found in San Francisco, Denver, Chicago, Atlanta, Indianapolis, and elsewhere.

Despite these successes there is one avenue that is not heavily traveled in junior and senior high school law-related education programs. There has been little integration of law content into obviously related courses. Economics, sociology, and anthropology courses have seldom included a law focus in their curricular design. It seems difficult to discuss economics in twentieth-century America without focusing on the regulatory role of government, yet this is often the case. Even in U.S. history the emphasis has not been on the law as a living instrument. Studying the Constitution as a historical document is certainly important, but even more important is measuring the impact of the living Constitution on our everyday lives. As the concern for law in schools grows, it seems reasonable that traditional courses will be re-examined with a legal focus.

The Content of Law Studies

Examples of content in a law-related curriculum have been described briefly in the previous chapter. This chapter will discuss more fully the content and concepts that are vital to students' understanding of the law in their lives. The object of law-related education is not to produce lawyers or inspire students to attend law school. It is to make them realize the ways in which the law affects people every day.

A common starting point (and frequently ending point) for law studies is demonstrating a need for laws or rules within all groups. Many materials focus on this area, and locally developed courses frequently use this approach as an introduction to law studies. The course in Park Forest Junior High School mentioned earlier is one example of this approach. The Park Forest course goes on to explore constitutional rights as the next step in understanding laws.

In Bellefonte, Pennsylvania, students at the senior high school have a choice of a number of minicourses, one of which, "The Constitution and Individual Rights," lays a foundation for understanding law.

The Street Law course in Washington, D.C., begins by asking a series of conceptual questions and then proceeds to answer them with problems, examples, and inquiry lessons. What is street law? What is law? What kinds of law are there? Where are laws made? All of these begin to whet students' interest in law and its effect on their lives.

A common classroom activity is to give the students a "mind walk." Students are asked to describe a typical day in their lives and then to hypothesize which of the activities they are engaged in are affected by legal constraints or legal protection. A variation on this device is to give students a list of situations where they have to pick out the activities that have legal impact and explain the impact. An example of such a mind walk is found on pages 18 and 19.

Mind Walk Exercise

Next to every daily activity, please make the following notations:

Place an X in either the yes or no spaces if you feel that the law (as you understand that term) does or does not affect that particular activity. If your response is yes, complete the next blank space by stating *how* the law affects the activity.

Activity	Any Legal Impact?		
	Yes	No	How?
1. Alarm clock awakens you. Turn on light.			
2. Use the bathroom.			
3. Wash face. Apply deodorant.			
4. Get dressed.			
5. Eat breakfast—cereal, milk, juice, eggs.			
6. Brush teeth.			
7. Read paper—see ad for TV sets on sale at store.			
8. Get in car.			
9. Drive to work.			
10. Stop at store on lunch hour to buy TV. Told it is a discontinued model, but better TV sets are available on easy credit terms.			
11. Get paid. Go to bank, cash check, deposit some of it.			

Activity	Any Legal Impact?		
	Yes	No	How?
12. Stop at grocery store to buy yogurt, vegetables, chicken, canned soup, canned tomatoes.			
13. Buy prescription at pharmacy.			
14. Stop at Sears. Buy stuffed animal for nephew. Pay with charge card.			
15. Go home; discover you have no heat. Call landlord.			
16. Listen to radio while you prepare dinner in electric oven.			
17. Eat dinner.			
18. Avon lady calls. You ask her in, buy $25 worth of cosmetics.			
19. Landlord phones to say pipes have burst but heat is on the way.			
20. Watch TV. Hear a noise near back door and call police.			
21. Police call is tape recorded.			
22. Police arrive, find back door jimmied but suspect gone.			
23. After difficult evening you bathe, wash hair.			
24. Turn out lights and go to bed.			

Other materials deal with the introduction to law or the basics of law. *More Means Less, A Concept Study of Conflict and its Resolution*, published as part of the Macmillan "Concepts for Social Studies" series, focuses on conflicts within groups and the need for laws to regulate and moderate these conflicts. The book examines American society and briefly discusses conflict resolution in other cultures. The examples used are from the legal practices of the Eskimos of East Greenland, the Ifugao of the Philippines, the Nuer people of the Sudan, the Ashanti of Ghana, and the Hopi of the southwest U.S.

Another excellent resource is the film, "Conflict Resolution Among the Kpelle—The Cows of Dolo Kem Paye," available from Holt, Rinehart and Winston. Filmed by anthropologist James Gibbs, the film provides a case study of how one culture resolves conflict. This film is appropriate for senior high school students and above. Other materials that offer a good introduction to law for students are cited in the Appendix to this fastback.

Another extremely popular law course is criminal law. Some schools focus on crime as part of a law course. Others offer a minicourse that may approach crime from a legal, sociological, and anthropological perspective. William Allen High School in Allentown, Pennsylvania, has offered such a minicourse; in it students look at crime as a social problem and examine the history and theory of punishment, police, courts, penal institutions, probation, and parole. Juvenile crime and delinquency are a particular focus. Current methods of treating youth offenders and the organization and function of agencies dealing with children and youth are studied. Finally, the causes, types, and effects of crime are examined.

Again, many commercial materials are available and useful for developing curricula in this area of law-related education. *The Criminal Law and You*, by Robert Sears, is part of Sadlier Oxford's "Oxford Spectrum" series and is a short volume useful in secondary schools. In organization and scope it is similar to books used in college criminology courses. The nature of crime, types of crimes, the role of the police, and the criminal trial are all covered in a very informative manner.

Crimes and Justice, part of Houghton Mifflin's "Justice in America" series, provides a breakdown of each type of crime with brief case examples, giving the student an opportunity to determine if, in his opinion, acts are criminal and why. This volume also focuses on criminal procedure and the role of the police. It is designed for junior high school use.

Two topics that are frequently incorporated into criminal law study are the police (law enforcement) and the correctional system. Study of the police and their role is vitally important to the student's understanding of criminal law. In many cities police serve in an atmosphere of almost constant stress. Often their interpretation of law enforcement will contradict the expectations of a community. Students in cities often feel that the police are harassing them. Many law-related courses are popular because students feel they are learning about an area that can help them "survive" on the street. The Street Law program is based on that premise. One of Scott Foresman's "People and the City" volumes, *You've Been Arrested,* is based on the same assumption. This book is written for junior high students with a low reading level. Another book designed for less able high school readers is *The Police,* one of the Xerox minibooks (see Appendix). The book looks at the role of the police but also sees policemen as individuals. It discusses proposals for improved police/community relations.

In some situations, one of the most difficult tasks in law-related education is helping students develop empathy for the police. An effective way of doing so is to arrange for older students to accompany police officers during their evening patrol. A less exciting but very effective method is to play the simulation game *Police Patrol,* which is produced by the Constitutional Rights Foundation. In most sessions of the game students become very aware of the difficult positions a police officer is put into. They come to appreciate the quick decisions he must make. If students enter the game with negative feelings about police officers, they lose many of them.

Another area of criminal law is the punishment and reform of criminals. There are a number of excellent published resources on the penal system, but perhaps most effective is the utilization of community resources such as a visit to local jails or county and state prisons. Other potential resources are discussed in the next section of this fastback.

Criminal law, then, may include study of the criminal mind;

81801

crimes and their definition; crime prevention (heavily police oriented); criminal trials (jury selection, plea bargaining, the role of defense and prosecuting attorneys, the role of the judge); and the punishment of criminals (prisons, halfway houses, probation, parole, capital punishment). The criminal statutes of a state are also often studied.

Juvenile law might be seen as an extension of criminal law, but because of the special treatment of juveniles in many states, juvenile law may best be studied separately. The Supreme Court decision *In re Gault* (1967) gave youths indicted for criminal acts the same rights as adults, but there are great variations among the states in handling juvenile criminals because of the nature of family and/or juvenile court systems. Only in recent years have states attempted to make juvenile courts more responsive to the legal rights of juvenile offenders and to society at large. Students can begin to explore the problems involved in rehabilitation efforts for juveniles, the theory of the juvenile court system, and the reasons behind the startling rise in juvenile crime.

One of the best (and most depressing) films on the juvenile court system is part of the "NBC White Paper" series, *This Child Is Rated 'X'*, which was filmed in several juvenile detention centers. It is not appropriate for students below junior high school. Other resources include two titles from the "Law in Action" series for grades 5-9, *Juvenile Problems and Law* and *Youth Attitudes and Police*. Materials in this area are less easily found, but there are some of excellent quality.

Most court cases (over 80%) are not criminal cases but civil cases not involving criminal actions. Civil law involves a number of concepts that are only vaguely familiar to most citizens. To initiate discussion with teachers and students on civil law and its effects, I often use the short true-false quiz on p. 24. The quiz deals, for the most part, with contracts, property, tort law, landlord/tenant relations, and civil procedure. Many of the questions, though seemingly unimportant, have a great deal to do with everyday life experiences in our country.

The nature of property can be studied at the local level by having students go to the courthouse and look up the grantor and grantee indices in the office of the recorder of deeds. Some students enjoy tracing the ownership of the land that they themselves live on; others trace the title of their school property or that of a favorite store. In the course of this study students can delve into the differing attitudes toward property that exist in various cultures. Our English-based idea of possessing real property was meaningless to American Indians, who found it absurd that someone could "possess" land. This mutual lack of understanding was the base for countless conflicts in the history of the United States. Understanding the legal concept of property can clarify many mystifying (to students) events in our nation's history.

Tort cases involve civil wrongs, that is, wrongs done through omission or commission that injure a citizen or his property in some way. Many involve damages of thousands of dollars.

Smaller claims (usually under $1,000) are settled in small claims courts where a judge listens to the case and makes a decision usually without an attorney representing the client. Students often become knowledgeable enough to sue in small claims court, which is often permissible with a parent present.

Contracts are a common source of dispute in small claims courts as well as in higher courts. A central question in these cases is, "Was there a contract?" Students may find themselves involved with contractual consumer cases when they buy defective merchandise. Consumer law is quite popular with students and teachers because of their direct involvement in purchasing products and services.

In New Holland, Pennsylvania, a teacher presents a case involving a young consumer who purchased a used car for $800. The odometer said 25,000 miles, but the dealer said that work had been done on the car to make it "like new." A week later the youth had work done on the car and the mechanic said the car had been driven at least 50,000 miles. The consumer sued for the return of $200. The car dealer claimed that everyone knew odometers were set back and that if he returned $200 he would make nothing on the car. Students are asked to render a verdict. The ensuing discussion pits consumerism versus free enterprise. Most students think that there is really a fraudulent misrepresentation of goods, even though they also think it is the dealer's right to make a profit. The teacher then sends students out to examine the claims of used car dealers as part of their next assignment.

Consumer law materials are readily available and many are excellent. Any teacher can utilize the magazine *Consumer Reports* as a ready resource. The Pennsylvania Department of Education has developed several good materials in consumer education. A fine film in this area, useful for both teachers and students, is *The Owl Who Gave a Hoot*. An animated cartoon, it centers around a series of consumer "rip-offs" and a wise owl who stops the fraudulent practices.

Many teachers and students are interested in constitutional law. A number of landmark decisions are commonly studied in junior and senior high classes. Students enjoy reading about the *Tinker* v. *Des Moines Independent Community School District* case dealing with two students who wore black armbands to school to protest the Vietnam war, because it has to do with the expression of dissent in public schools.

Other areas of law commonly covered are environmental law, court procedure and trials, the role of attorneys, international law, and family law. The bibliographies available from the ABA are quite helpful in identifying specific materials. In addition, both the *Bill of Rights Newsletter*, published by the Constitutional Rights Foundation, and *Law in American Society* have thematic issues covering some of these areas.

The Law—What Do <u>You</u> Know?*

T or F   1. Robbery and burglary are the same thing.

T or F   2. If you are found not guilty of criminal assault, you cannot be tried again in a civil case.

T or F   3. An oral contract is not legally binding unless there are at least two witnesses.

T or F   4. If you are mistakenly sued for an act that you did not do, you need not reply to the complaint.

T or F   5. Punitive damages are the difference between actual and estimated damages.

T or F   6. A jury may be composed of fewer than 12 people.

Answers are found on page 41.

T or F	7.	Asking for a change of venue means you wish a new trial.
T or F	8.	A title search is still illegal in many states.
T or F	9.	You cannot sue the police for false imprisonment.
T or F	10.	Intestate refers to legal relations of people with a state.
T or F	11.	A deposition can only be given in an open courtroom.
T or F	12.	The right to a jury trial may be waived if a party does not demand it in a civil suit.
T or F	13.	In order to be legally operative, it is necessary that an offer contain all the terms of the contract to be made.
T or F	14.	If you have the highest bid at an auction, you must be sold the item you bid on.
T or F	15.	If you change the terms of an offer in your acceptance, you can be found in breach of contract.
T or F	16.	Lawyers are not allowed to represent a client in small claims court in Pennsylvania.
T or F	17.	Amicus curiae refers to the plaintiff's lawyer.
T or F	18.	In order to be convicted in a criminal case, a person must be guilty beyond a reasonable doubt.
T or F	19.	A corporation cannot be sued without the consent of the attorney general of the state where the corporation is located.
T or F	20.	A clause stating that you cannot sublet your apartment without the consent of the landlord is legally enforceable.

Community Resources for Law Study

I have emphasized throughout this fastback that effective law-related education requires extensive use of community resources. In this section a brief description and discussion of some prominent community resources will be presented. The list of resources will not be exhaustive nor will each resource be found in every community. The list will, however, be a useful starting point for discovering each individual community's resources for law-related education.

Local resources are frequently more useful than remote resources, despite the possibility of the latter having more notoriety. I recently worked with a group of educators and justice officials who wished to initiate a law-related teacher training program in their community. The group kept trying to find well-known individuals in the state to come to their workshop. Finally, one educator said that if law-related education programs are supposed to utilize local resources, then this teacher training workshop should act as a model in doing just that, rather than searching outside the community for assistance.

An obvious human resource is attorneys. Many attorneys are eager and willing to help teachers because of their interest in this type of citizenship education. The ABA, the major organization of the legal profession, has accepted the obligation to help make an understanding of our legal system an essential goal of elementary and secondary education. Attorneys may not agree on the precise method of achieving this goal, but most would support it.

What can attorneys do to contribute to law-related education? One obvious action is to come into classrooms and interact with students over questions of law. Teachers should be cautious, however. Attorneys may come into a class and overwhelm the students with facts or bore them with droning explanations. This need not happen, however, if the teacher makes it clear to the attorney what is desired in the class presentation and what to expect from the students. Teachers need not feel timid about giving instructions to an attorney. Most of them, when asked to come to a classroom, respond by saying, "I'd be glad to come. What do you want me to do?"

Attorneys can do a variety of things. They might discuss a point of law that is currently under discussion by the class, or they might speak on a wide range of law areas, including the law as a career.

An attorney might also serve as a board member of, or a consultant to, a joint school-community committee planning law-related education programs.

Preparing briefs and conducting mock trials are two classroom activities in which attorneys can be helpful. Students often are asked to brief a case, much as an attorney would. The briefing consists of presenting the following data: the title of the case, the facts that raised the legal question, the issues, previous decisions in similar cases, and the case decision and its rationale. By acting out major issues in a mock trial, students derive a better understanding of important concepts than they would if they were only to read about them in a textbook. An attorney may act as the judge in such cases or serve as the advisor to the students preparing briefs for such a trial.

Courthouse personnel are another community resource for familiarizing students with the functions of a courthouse. If a class wishes to visit a courthouse in a city, the teacher would be wise to inquire which courtrooms are best to visit on a particular day. In a rural area choices are much more limited, so the teacher should check with the clerk of the court to find what day might be educationally profitable for the class. The clerk can aid the teacher in making these arrangements, but a personal letter or telephone call should be made to the judge to remind him of the visit and thank him for his cooperation.

For the most part, judges are quite pleased to have students in the courtroom. They may stop a case briefly to explain to the class what they are doing procedurally and why. After the court session the judge may entertain questions, give students a tour of the court, or ask the students some questions. If their schedule permits, judges may be able to come to the school to aid the students and teachers in their case study or mock trials.

In addition to the clerk of the court and the judge, a key person in a county courthouse is the recorder of deeds. The recorder can show students the grantor and grantee books that trace the chain of a property title from first recording to the present.

Another courtroom that might be more convenient to visit is the local court of the magistrate or justice of the peace. In most states cases in these courts are limited in terms of maximum sentences and damage decrees. The courts are quite flexible, however, and many magistrates can schedule a person's case at a convenient time for a class visit. There are no formal arguments by attorneys in these courts, so schedules are easily accommodated to class time. In most courts of this size, civil cases are limited to a $500 or $1,000 maximum for damages, and neither party can be represented by counsel. Thus the proceeding is much simpler, and students would have a better likelihood of following along.

A very visible community resource is the police force. Many larger departments have a community relations officer who can come to class and discuss the role of the police with students. In elementary schools this procedure is often limited to the officer visiting the class and lecturing. Proper preparation for the police officer's visit is essential. Students might gather pictures of police at work, observe police in their community, or ask parents or other adults about the police officer's work. Then when the officer comes, students will be more attentive listeners and informed questioners. This type of preparation, however, is not necessary only for the police officer's visit. It is necessary to make such preparations before the visit of any classroom guest.

In addition to the classroom visit, a trip to a police station is often very useful. It may be possible to arrange for older students to accompany the police on patrol. If not, the teacher might go on a police ride-along in order to become familiar with the problems of police patrol. Police stations usually have a local jail or holding cells in the same complex. These can be visited as part of the trip to the station.

Because of the nature of prisons, careful preparations are necessary before taking a class to visit one. First, the warden or assistant warden should be contacted; then the teacher should conduct a "dry run" of the exact trip planned for the students. Ask questions about prison procedures, since this type of information will be useful to the students. Inquire about the possibility of a prisoner talking with the students. If a prisoner is available for conversation, he should be warned that "preaching" to youth is usually ineffective. An open discussion will generally be a much more effective deterrent to students contemplating crime than a moralistic sermon. Invite the warden (if his schedule permits) to discuss with the students the philosophy of the correctional institution.

Upon release, many prisoners are under the supervision of parole officers. These social welfare personnel (probation officers, youth service workers, welfare case workers) provide a unique view of a system that is trying to rehabilitate those who served time in prison. Social service workers are usually quite willing to come to talk to a class of students. They also may be helpful in getting a small group of students permission to visit more inaccessible places, such as a maximum security prison.

Some other community resource persons bear mention. Consumer advocates can provide an interesting perspective for students interested in consumer law and consumer rights. A consumer advocate might also help a teacher in planning a field trip to see consumer rights in action.

If a school is in an area where there is a college or university, a faculty anthropologist or ecologist might be available to provide understandings in comparative or environmental law. These people might also have materials they have developed that could be used in the classroom. With some advance notice they will probably be available to visit a classroom.

Some other useful human resources in a community include building inspectors, bankers, tax lawyers, FBI agents, real estate agents, law students, representatives of various federal government agencies, IRS agents, and landlords.

Introducing a Law-Related Curriculum in Your Community

How do you begin to get law-related education into your school? Here are some suggestions for getting started.

Begin by gathering materials on law-related education and reviewing them. The brief bibliography in this fastback is a start. Most of the works cited have additional bibliographies. Popular news magazines like *Time* and *Newsweek* have sections devoted to law and justice. These sections can start an interested reader on a hunt for further useful information about the law. Check the Tuesday newspapers. Supreme Court decisions are read on Monday and reported extensively in the Tuesday newspapers. They can serve as a more up-to-date file of law in America than any published material available.

Next, write to the American Bar Association for its series of working notes on various aspects of law-related education. These notes provide various views of law-related education, print and audiovisual resources, and ideas for curriculum development. The working notes available from ABA free or for a nominal charge are:

Reflections on Law-Related Education
    Composed of brief views by Joel Henning, Isidore Starr, and Earl Morris, among others, all of whom have been involved in law-related education; (1973, free).

Directory of Law-Related Educational Activities
    Describes more than 250 projects around the country. Some of the material is outdated; much has happened since publication in 1974. Useful, nevertheless; (free).

Bibliography of Law-Related Curriculum Materials: Annotated
Descriptions of more than 1,000 books and pamphlets for classrooms, K-12, and teacher reference. Included are novels, essays, and plays, in addition to more usual curriculum materials; (1976, $1).

Media: An Annotated Catalogue of Law-Related Audio-Visual Materials
Describes more than 400 films, filmstrips, and tapes for classroom use and teacher reference, with addresses and prices for sale and rental; (1975, $1).

Gaming: An Annotated Catalogue of Law-Related Games and Simulations
Describes over 100 games and simulations for classroom use. The number of players and time needed for each game are given; a brief commentary on simulation as a teaching method by Todd Clark is also included; (1975, $1).

The $$ Game: A Guidebook on the Funding of Law-Related Educational Programs
A valuable book for those interested in developing a long-range program in law-related education; includes information on funding sources, writing funding proposals, securing community support, and institutionalizing programs. Some of the funding sources suggested have dried up; nevertheless, the overall presentation is very useful; (1975, $1).

Law-Related Education in America: Guidelines for the Future
An extensive study of the nature of law-related education—structure, goals, teaching materials, and funding, with a lengthy appendix of useful information on grants and projects; (1975, $2).

Teaching Teachers About Law: A Guide to Law-Related Teacher Education Programs
A series of articles on various models of inservice teacher education efforts in law. Ideas for developing programs are offered as well as program descriptions. Though repetitious at times, this book is readable and timely; (1976, $2).

After one reviews the ideas and suggestions from the ABA series and other materials, it is time to solicit support from the community, the local school board, and the state department of education. The state department may be able to tell you of successful law studies programs in your state, suggest means of support, or offer to work with you in developing a model program. School boards can offer support by merely endorsing a program in law-related education. With just that support, a community will look more favorably upon such a program. Another way a school board can aid in the development of such a program is by allowing the use of school facilities for meetings or workshops to promote the program. Finally, the school board might be able to provide funds for such a program through a local budget allocation or by applying to state or federal agencies for funds.

Community support and resources are necessary to achieve a successful law studies program. Community people, such as an interested attorney, a principal, a teacher, a police officer (either the chief or the community relations officer would be best), and a local teacher educator would be key personnel to serve on a planning committee for a law studies program. Other possible members of such a committee might be a social worker, a parole officer, or an interested public official. The function of this committee is planning the direction and content of the law studies program in the local area. This model has been successfully implemented to promote law-related education in 12 regions of Pennsylvania. A community-based committee can best assay the resources of a community and can encourage other community people and institutions to cooperate in the successful development of a local law studies program.

Other valuable resources are the already established law education projects. Some of these are national in scope but have regional offices. It may be most expeditious for a school district to base its program on successfully established projects rather than attempt to design a totally new curriculum. One such source is the Institute for Political and Legal Education (IPLE), which is based in New Jersey. IPLE has developed project materials, both print and audiovisual, on voter education, government, and law. In addition, it disseminates materials on staff development and evaluation.

If you are located in an area that has a law school nearby, the Street Law project may be of interest to you. The course is generally taught by law students who receive credit for their teaching. The law students concentrate on presenting the law from a practical point of view. The Street Law project has been sponsored by some of the outstanding law schools in the country. If a school district is interested in this approach, it should contact the National Street Law Institute.

In contrast to the practical approach of the Street Law project is the more theoretical approach of the Law in a Free Society project, a civic education program of the State Bar of California. This program is based on eight concepts considered fundamental to an understanding of social and political life: authority, responsibility, privacy, justice, property, freedom, diversity, and participation. Law in a Free Society has produced excellent materials for classroom use and also works in teacher training and program development.

The Constitutional Rights Foundation (CRF), based in Los Angeles, has developed a program called Law, Education, and Participation (LEAP) that assists communities in the development of law-related education programs through conferences and teacher/student workshops. LEAP has offices in St. Louis and Philadelphia.

The Law in American Society Foundation (LIASF) probably has the largest and longest running summer training institutes in law-related education. Begun over 10 years ago, LIASF now sponsors projects in over 30 colleges and universities, 15 city school districts, and six prison systems.

Descriptions of other projects having useful materials and suggestions can be found in the ABA *Directory of Law-Related Education Activities* or by writing the Special Committee on Youth Education for Citizenship of the ABA directly.

A most important consideration at the early stages of planning is funding. In addition to the school district, local or state bar associations should be contacted as possible sources of support. Service organizations such as Kiwanis and Lions may also provide materials or support.

Some states, like Pennsylvania, have regional justice commissions. Usually their funds are earmarked for specific purposes. If public education is one of their interests, they too, should be approached for funding. Many law education projects were originally funded by the federal Law Enforcement Association Administration, but now those funds are channeled through the individual states. So depending on the state, money may or may not be available for law-related projects from this source.

A better prospect for funding is the U.S. Office of Education. Under Title IV-C of the Elementary and Secondary Education Act, funds are available to districts for innovative programs. Recently the Allegheny Intermediate Unit in Pittsburgh received a large grant under Title IV-C for the promotion of law-related education in elementary schools. If a district feels that a law program may promote intergroup relations, it may be eligible for Title I funds.

Nonprofit foundations also have contributed to law-related education. Some of the foundations that have contributed in the past include the American Bar Endowment, the Carnegie Foundation, the Danforth Foundation, the Ford Foundation, the Lilly Endowment, the Rockefeller Foundation, and the New York Foundation.

The Prospect for Law-Related Programs in Schools

All signs at this time seem to indicate that law-related education will continue to grow and prosper. Educators have become more sensitive to community needs and to community resources. A program that involves the community will usually continue to be supported by that community.

Local bar associations and individual attorneys are concerned about issues like the rising rate of juvenile crime and the lack of understanding by citizens of their basic rights and responsibilities. Most attorneys that I have dealt with in workshops have been only too happy to visit classes to discuss these issues. Many have asked to come back. One assistant district attorney spent all day in school, then asked if he could return later for two full days. Attorneys frequently find teaching children and youth to be a pleasant and exhilarating change from trials or legal research.

Another positive sign is the support from other members of the justice community such as police, judges, prison officials, probation officers, and others who have been generous in contributing time and effort toward a broader understanding of our system of justice.

An indication that law-related education will continue to grow in popularity is the continued prospect of funding. Both government and private sources have seen the value of law-related education and have poured thousands of dollars into the program. This is likely to continue, although the funds will probably be distributed more selectively than they were before. Local bar associations and the American Bar Association have been directly involved in promoting law-related education as one of their major service areas and have been generous in their funding. Furthermore, they have been getting other groups and individuals interested in the support of law-related education.

Recent surveys have indicated that the public is pleased with the attention to law studies in the curriculum and is willing to back continued programs in this area. Currently the emphasis for such programs has been at the secondary school level. In the future there will likely be a concerted effort to introduce and promote the concepts of law at all levels of the curriculum.

A continuing need will be in the area of teacher training. The summer workshop model has been successful in the past and more workshops will be offered over the next four or five years. Even more important is preservice teacher training. Currently, law-related education is not offered in social studies methods classes unless the instructor has a special interest in law studies. With more funds and materials becoming available, institutions will be able to offer components in their methods classes on law-related education. A recent conference in Pennsylvania sought to expose methods professors from every teacher training institution in the state to the nature and content of law-related education. The professors produced modules on the subject and formed consortia to share materials and ideas on law-related education. The Pennsylvania experience will possibly become a model for other states.

It seems, then, that law-related education will become a major concern in teacher training, and in turn will become a common component of the school curriculum. This statement is based on both statistical inference and my personal hope. That hope is that all students in this country will be able to understand the reasons for the laws in our society. Only through this understanding will we be able to produce a truly involved and concerned citizenry.

Appendix

Useful Addresses and Materials

American Bar Association
Special Committee on Youth Education for Citizenship
1155 East 60th
Chicago, IL 60637
> Handles eight current publications (see page 30) and other information.

Peter Senn, Executive Director
Law in American Society Foundation
33 North LaSalle Street
Chicago, IL 60602
> Provides information on workshops and many useful back editions of *Law in American Society*.

Vivian Monroe, Executive Director
Constitutional Rights Foundation
6310 San Vincente Boulevard
Los Angeles, CA 90048
> Provides information on workshops, publishes *Bill of Rights Newsletter*, sponsors the Law Education and Participation (LEAP) offices in St. Louis and Philadelphia, and produces excellent materials like *The Jury Game*, *Police Patrol*, and *Kids in Crisis*.

David Whitney, Director
Correctional Service of Minnesota
1427 Washington Avenue South
Minneapolis, MN 55454

Acts as a clearinghouse for recent print materials and many films; also produces some excellent materials like the multimedia kit, "America's Prisons."

Lee Arbetman, Education Director
National Street Law Institute
605 G Street, N.W.
Washington, DC 20001
Produces materials, trains law students for public school teaching of law studies, provides consultants and information.

Charles Quigley, Executive Director
Law in a Free Society
606 Wilshire Boulevard, Suite 600
Santa Monica, CA 90401
Produces multimedia materials, provides workshops for pre- and inservice teacher training.

Barry Lefkowitz, Director
Institute for Political and Legal Education
P.O. Box 426
Pitman, NJ 08071
Produces materials; organizes workshops for teacher training in voter education, government, and law.

Teacher Materials

The Methods Book
   Arlene Gallagher, et al.
   Strategies for Law-Focused Education
   Law in American Society Foundation, 1977
   33 North LaSalle Street
   Chicago, IL 60602

Teaching About the Law
   Ronald Gerlach and Lynne Lamprecht
   W. H. Anderson Co., 1977
   646 Main Street
   Cincinnati, OH 45201

Law-Related Education Competencies
   Pennsylvania Department of Education
   Box 911
   Harrisburg, PA 17126

Consumer Education Competencies
   Pennsylvania Department of Education
   Box 911
   Harrisburg, PA 17126

Values, Law-Related Education, and the Elementary School Teacher
   David Naylor
   National Education Association, 1976
   Order Department
   Academic Building
   Saw Mill Road
   West Haven, CT 06516

School District Materials

Law-Related Education: A Teacher Resource
Office of Curriculum and Instruction
The School District of Philadelphia
Parkway at 21st Street
Philadelphia, PA 19103

Law-Related Educational Unit
Park Forest Junior High School
State College, PA 16801

Student Materials

Crimes and Justice, Law and the City, Poverty and Welfare, Landlord and Tenant, Youth and the Law
"Justice in America" Series
Houghton Mifflin (Boston)

Great Cases of the Supreme Court, Law in a New Land, Vital Issues of the Constitution
"Trailmarks of Liberty" Series
Houghton Mifflin (Boston)
Developed by the Law in American Society Foundation

Buyer Beware, You've Been Arrested
"People and the City" Series
Scott, Foresman & Company (Glenview, Ill.)
Two books dealing directly with law-related education

The American Legal System
Ginn & Company, Xerox Publishing Division (Lexington, Mass.)
Developed by the Cornell Law Project

Courts and the Law, Liberty Under Law, The Supreme Court, The Penal System, The Police
American Education Publications, Xerox Publishing Division (Columbus, Oh.)
Five unit books on law

Racial Equality, Woman and the Law, Due Process of Law, Rights of Privacy, Religious Freedom, Freedom of Speech
"To Protect These Rights" Series
National Textbook Company (Skokie, Ill.)
Published in conjunction with the American Civil Liberties Union

Juvenile Problems and Law, Youth Attitudes and Police, Lawmaking, Courts and Trials, Young Consumers
"Law in Action" Series
West Publishing Co. (St. Paul, Minn.)

American Presidency, American Judicial System, Congress—The National Legislature, Governments and Politics in Today's World, The Criminal Law and You
"Oxford Spectrum" Series
Sadlier Oxford (New York)
Five books with a law-related focus

Three excellent films not in the American Bar Association media bibliography are:

The Owl Who Gave a Hoot (1967)
National A. V. Center, General Services Administration (Washington, D.C.)
A consumer education cartoon

The Cows of Dolo Dem Paye (1969)
Holt, Rinehart & Winston (New York)
On law among the Kpelle of Liberia

This Child is Rated 'X' (1971)
"NBC White Paper" Series

Other excellent materials are available. Those mentioned here do not reflect the author's endorsement so much as his familiarity with the materials.

Answers to quiz on pp. 24 & 25. 1. F. 2. F. 3. F. 4. F. 5. F. 6. T. 7. F. 8. F. 9. F. 10. F. 11. F. 12. T.
13. T. 14. F. 15. F. 16. T. 17. F. 18. F. 19. F. 20. T.